BONJOUR BITCHES!

EVERYONE BRINGS JOY INTO THIS OFFICE, SOME WHEN THEY ENTER AND OTHERS WHEN THEY LEAVE

I AM NOT FEELING VERY WORKY TODAY

I USED TO BE LIKE YOU, HAPPY AND FULL OF LIFE

MY FAVOURITE CO-WORKER IS THE COFFEE MACHINE

THIS JOB IS TAKING UP MY TIME TO JOB SEARCH

I ACTIVELY AVOID OFFICE POLITICS BY HATING EVERYONE EQUALLY

MY BIGGEST CONTRIBUTION TO WORKPLACE SAFETY IS HAVING A CUP OF COFFEE IN THE MORNING

HOW THE HELL DO YOU STILL WORK HERE?

HERE'S TO ANOTHER DAY OF OUTWARD SMILES AND INWARD SCREAMS

LET ME DROP EVERYTHING AND WORK ON YOUR FREAKING PROBLEM

I'M SORRY, DID THE MIDDLE OF MY SENTENCE INTERRUPT THE BEGINNING OF YOURS?

MAY THE BRIDGES I BURN LIGHT THE WAY

I SURVIVED ANOTHER MEETING THAT COULD HAVE BEEN AN EMAIL

IF IDIOTS COULD FLY, THIS PLACE WOULD BE AN AIRPORT

**I DON'T KNOW
I JUST WORK
HERE**

I DON'T ALWAYS FART AT MY DESK. BUT WHEN I DO, EVERYONE WANTS TO COME TALK TO ME

I'D LOVE TO HELP YOU WHEN YOU ARE BACK ON YOUR MEDS

MY BRAIN HAS TOO MANY TABS OPEN

SOMETIMES I MAY TURN UP FOR WORK A LITTLE 'TIRED AND EMOTIONAL'

**NOT MY CIRCUS
NOT MY MONKEYS**

AUTOCORRECT CAN GO TO HE'LL

I WOULD AGREE WITH YOU... BUT THEN WE WOULD BOTH BE WRONG.

I APPLAUD YOUR EFFORTS TO SAVE WATER BUT REALLY, YOU CAN FLUSH THE TOILET

YOU TYPE LOUDER THAN A HAIL STORM ON A TIN ROOF

I KNEW WE WOULD NEVER BE FRIENDS WHEN YOU LEFT THE WASHROOM WITHOUT WASHING YOUR HANDS

I'M ONLY RESPONSIBLE FOR WHAT I SAY, NOT WHAT YOU UNDERSTAND

YOU MUST BE EXHAUSTED FROM WATCHING ME DO EVERYTHING

ONE WEEK THEY LOVE YOU. NEXT WEEK THEY HATE YOU. BOTH WEEKS, I GET PAID

WHAT IS THE HR-APPROVED WAY TO TELL CO-WORKERS THEY ARE STUPID?

**COFFEE
BLAH BLAH BLAH
DRIVE HOME
WINE**

I HAVE TERRIBLE IDEAS IF YOU NEED ANY

IF IT REQUIRES FAKE SMILING, I PROBABLY WON'T COME

I THINK, THEREFORE WE HAVE NOTHING IN COMMON

TODAY IS NOT YOUR DAY. TOMORROW DOESN'T LOOK GOOD EITHER

WHEN I ASK FOR DIRECTIONS, PLEASE DON'T USE WORDS LIKE 'EAST'

AH, THE SOUND OF FAKE LAUGHTER. I MUST STILL BE AT WORK

**2 WORDS
1 FINGER**

IN MY DEFENCE, I WAS LEFT UNSUPERVISED

IT'S THE VILLAGE, THEY WANT THEIR IDIOT BACK

I'M SORRY...DID I ROLL MY EYES TOO LOUD?

I GET MOST OF MY EXERCISE THESE DAYS FROM SHAKING MY HEAD IN DISBELIEF

I HAVE NEITHER THE TIME NOR CRAYONS TO EXPLAIN THIS TO YOU

I CAME
I SAW
I LEFT EARLY

I'M FEELING A BIT OVERWORKED AND A BIT UNDER-INTOXICATED

I'M NOT THE TYPE OF PERSON YOU SHOULD PUT ON SPEAKER PHONE

HEY ELSA? THE COLD ACTUALLY BOTHERS THE REST OF US

IF MY MOUTH DOESN'T SAY IT, MY FACE DEFINITELY WILL

PEOPLE NEED TO START APPRECIATING THE EFFORT I PUT IN TO NOT BE A SERIAL KILLER

I DON'T GET ENOUGH CREDIT FOR THE FACT THAT I DO ALL THIS SOBER

Printed by Amazon Italia Logistica S.r.l.
Torrazza Piemonte (TO), Italy